THE Best Bug Parade

by Stuart J. Murphy · illustrated by Holly Keller

HarperCollins*Publishers*

To Nancy—who makes my life a parade
—S.J.M.

For Lily Lawrence
—H.K.

The illustrations in this book were done with pen and ink, watercolor, and pastel on Rives BFK.

For information address HarperCollins Children's Books, a division of
HarperCollins Publishers, 195 Broadway, New York, NY 10007.

Bugs incorporated in the MathStart series design were painted by Jon Buller.

HarperCollins®, ♟®, and MathStart® are registered trademarks of HarperCollins Publishers Inc.

The Best Bug Parade
Text copyright © 1996 by Stuart J. Murphy
Illustrations copyright © 1996 by Holly Keller
Manufactured in China. All rights reserved.

Library of Congress Cataloging-in-Publication Data
Murphy, Stuart J., date
  The best bug parade / by Stuart J. Murphy ; illustrated by Holly
Keller.
        p.   cm. (MathStart. Level 1)
  Summary: A variety of different bugs compare their relative sizes while
going on parade.
  ISBN 0-06-025871-3. — ISBN 0-06-025872-1 (lib. bdg.)
  ISBN 0-06-446700-7 (pbk.)
  [1. Insects—Fiction.   2. Size—Fiction.   3. Parades—Fiction.
4. Stories in rhyme.]   I. Keller, Holly, ill.   II. Title.   III. Series.
PZ8.3.M935Be   1996   94-49316
[E]—dc20   CIP
                                                                   AC

Typography by Elynn Cohen
21 22 23 SCP 35 34 33 32
❖

The Best Bug Parade

I am big.

I am bigger than you are.

7

I am the biggest bug by far.

Big. Bigger! Biggest!!

9

I am small.

I am smaller than small.

19

Bug Parade

20

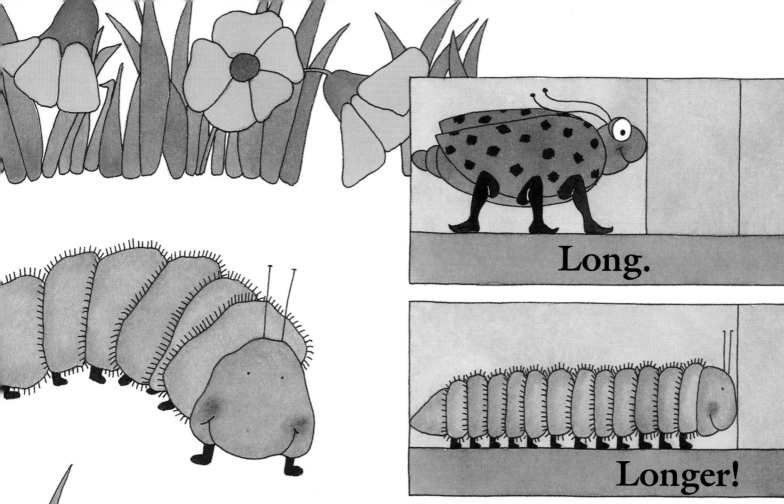

Long.

Longer!

But I am the longest bug in view.

Longest!!

I am short.

I am shorter than short.

24

I am the shortest bug of this sort.

Short.

Shorter!

Shortest!!

29

When we are all together,
long and short, big and small,

we are not just good or better,

we are . . .

I f you would like to have fun with the math concepts presented in *The Best Bug Parade*, here are a few suggestions:

- Read the story with the child and describe what is going on in each picture. Ask questions throughout the story, such as "Do the bugs look the same or do they look different?" and "How do they look different?"

- Together, draw and color some of your own imaginary bugs. Then cut them out and help the child arrange them in order of size. Line them up for your own best bug parade.

- Gather some toys—such as cars, blocks, dolls, or teddy bears—and ask the child to arrange them in order of size. Discuss them with the child using the vocabulary from the book. For example: "Which toy is longer?" "Which is longest?" You can even make another parade.

- Look at things in the real world—family members, pets, furniture, plates, flowers—and discuss their size relationships. "Who is bigger?" "Which is smallest?" Extend the concept by asking such questions as "Which is older?" "Which is youngest?" "Which is darker?" "Which is lightest?"

Following are some activities that will help you extend the concepts presented in *The Best Bug Parade* into a child's everyday life.

Cooking: Compare measuring spoons, cups, and bowls while cooking together.

Nature: Take a tape measure or ruler and compare plants in your garden or a nearby park.

Games: Use the vocabulary "Long—Longer—Longest" and "Short—Shorter—Shortest" to discuss the distance a ball is kicked or thrown. Play penny toss on the sidewalk and measure each toss to prove which is longer, shortest, etc.

The following books include some of the same concepts that are presented in *The Best Bug Parade*:

- IS IT LARGER? IS IT SMALLER? by Tana Hoban

- TITCH by Pat Hutchins

- SUPER SUPER SUPERWORDS by Bruce McMillan